BLUE REQUIEM

ALSO BY DEVREAUX BAKER

Hungry Ghosts
out of the bones of earth
Red Willow People
Beyond the Circumstance of Sight
Light at the Edge

Editor-in-chief,
Spirit of Place: Mendocino County Women Poets Anthology

co-editor (with Sharon Doubiago and Susan Maeder),
Wood, Water, Air and Fire, The Anthology of Mendocino Women Poets

BLUE REQUIEM

poems

by

Devreaux Baker

Wild Ocean Press
San Francisco
www.wildoceanpress.com

Copyright 2026 by Devreaux Baker
All rights reserved

Grateful acknowledgement to The San Diego Poetry Annual, 2024-2025 where "Body of the Beloved" first appeared as winner of the 2024 Steve Kowit Poetry Prize.

"Blue Requiem" was winner of the Willie Morris Award for Southern Writing for Poetry. A limited-edition broadside was commissioned by the University of Mississippi, Oxford for the Oxford Conference of the Book.

"Big River Adagio" was published in *Spirit of Place: Mendocino County Women Poets Anthology*, 2025, Wayfind Press.

Cover design by Solange Roberdeau
Cover artwork by Fritz Horstman, *Folded Cyanotype 227*, 2023. Cyanotype fluid on paper, 9 ½ x 9 ½ in. Image ©Fritz Horstman, 2025. Fritz Horstman is represented by Municipal Bonds, San Francisco, CA. Used with permission of the Artist.
Author photograph by Amy Scharmann/Sidekick Photography

Blue Requiem / Devreaux Baker-1st ed.
ISBN: 978-1-941137-16-1

Printed in the United States of America

For Barry

Contents

BLUE REQUIEM
Body of the Beloved	3
What Have We Got To Lose	5
After the Diagnosis	6
Blue Requiem	8
Mississippi 4 AM	10
The Swimmers	12
Mapping	13
Inviting Death In	14
Mendocino Shuffle	16
Ides of March	17
Freedom	18
Heart Failure	19
The Morning We First Met	20
Queen Bitch	22
Garden Elegy	23
Archeology of Us	24
Soul of the Thing	25
Runaway Horses	26
Big River Adagio	28
Bodhisattva Blues	30
This Time Around	32
Ghosts Everywhere	34
Holding On and Letting Go	35
Visible Horizon	36
Groundswell (for M.K.)	37
Incantation for a Healing	38

THE WOMAN REMEMBERS SHE IS A RIVER
Dream Journal	43
Suminagashi. (for S.R.)	44
Greece	45
Moonglow Over the Rio Hondo	46
Welcoming The New Year	48
Twenty-Two States on the Other Side of Life	50

Disappearing	51
Pleiades	52
We Heard Water	53
The Angel of Life	54
Water Binds Me to You	55
What Abides	56
Return To Taos	57
Becoming The Street	59
Finding a Cure for Cancer	61
Heartmoor	63
The Woman Remembers She is a River	64

Blue Requiem

Life will break you. Nobody can protect you from that, and living alone won't either, for solitude will also break you with its yearning. You have to love. You have to feel it. It is the reason you are here on earth. You are here to risk your heart. You are here to be swallowed up.

Louise Erdrich, *The Painted Drum*

Body of the Beloved

The morning the roof caught on fire we were not speaking.
I forget now what happened. It could have been a tone of voice
that made me think I was drowning.

Could have been a held resentment, entering me like something
familiar, rising in dark water, swelling higher and higher
until all my seasons were storms and I was a hurricane.

For whatever reason when the house caught on fire
we were not speaking until I heard you call my name,
saw the flames roaring up from the roof and called 911.

But the wait for the fire department was too long,
you and your son climbed that roof and put out the fire.
I watched you standing up there, mythic in all that smoke

and thought how it took the damn house bursting into flame
to make me swear I was done with small things that could never
match the sight of your body stepping out of smoke and fire,

clothes black with ash, hands burned.

When you climbed back down, I looked at your face and saw you
as though for the first time, felt you in me, like a great thirst
and knew this is our meeting place, beyond measurement, beyond

beauty and terror, where blood loves the way of veins and darkness
becomes light, where there are no road signs and ghost deer drift
with smoking hooves.

This is the crossroads where we meet face to face and I say
I can bear this life full of constant returning from the edge
of despair or disaster, if you are there, waiting,

where living is all we want and I am stunned with the
lips and hands, eyes and fingers, arms, legs and heart
of the body of my beloved once again.

What Have We Got To Lose

When the fox ran in front of my car I stopped and saw
she stopped too at the edge of the road, was looking me in the eye.
I rolled the window down thinking she would run now, but she
stood, paws rooted like a firm apostrophe of fur

in a magical realism tale about women and foxes
and searched my face for something. Food? She looked thin.
Was she hungry? Why wasn't she frightened of the car, motor
running, of the window rolling down, of the woman leaning out.

I had been so angry all morning at the mail for not coming,
at my daughter for not calling, at my husband for an unexpected
dark look, when I was filled to the brim with my own dark looks.
But here I was, almost home again, lugging that load of

fuck this shit world attitude back home with me when the fox
crossed the road. Everything left me then like a dark wind
in a country western song. I took a deep breath and breathed in
that brave fox, the green trees, your life and mine tangled on the
floor of our house.

I breathed in what we create together in this world.
Breathed in the hard with the soft, the found heart-ache,
the lost redemption, the forgetful and forgotten everyday
world weariness of the two of us, that makes us cling

to the tangle of your life knotting itself with mine, of my life
throwing out nets, pulling our bodies back in, shaking the woven
ropes free of saltwater tears, whispering, Oh baby
what have we got to lose?

After the Diagnosis

After the diagnosis I spent months visiting the hospital green room
wrapped in a blue paper gown sitting in a row with other women
waiting to have our sentencing read from a surgeon judge
just inside closed doors.

I would lean back in my chair and think about having sex with you
think about your body swimming across lifetimes to sink into mine.
I would close my eyes and imagine your chest beneath my hands
filled with its dark tributaries of soul, the two of us swimming from

blindness into sight, creating speech with our eyes and hands,
covering ourselves with molecules of life that transcended pain or
trauma. Together we became soft and brave, we became twins
joined at the clavicle, joined at the breastbone, joined at the hip.

In the hospital green room, I would hold the image of us in my
mouth, probe it with the tip of my tongue, as though it was sacred.
I would make love to it and give it a shape beyond words
until it was filled with its own dark grace, powerful beyond flesh
or blood.

The stellar beauty our two bodies created became a panther
in my mind, gave me strength, made me untouchable
by their metal devices. I lay on the examining table those days
having sex in my mind while they stood over me, in a world
of white clinical terms and coded hospital language,

exploring the terrain of my body, wandering the outer reaches
like lost arctic explorers, stopping now and then to discuss
the shape or texture of tundra, while I lay naked beneath them,
slick and wet with the sweat of your body, the smell of your hair,
the taste of your hands.

Fear moved past me then like a giant puppet in a Oaxacan
wedding parade, made of sticks and painted paper
bouncing and bobbing like a bad dream until, torn and shredded
from wind or rain, it disappeared when morning came.

Blue Requiem

Tonight, the sounds of my neighbor's bass guitar
remind me that the blues come from some geography
of the wandering spirit like Odysseus forever searching
for the way home again.

The journeys of body and soul always begin in unlikely places
from ancient deserts filled with the arc and curve of war-time flares
or drumbeats of nomadic tribes, to bay water shacks of gumbo kings
anxious to elevate lives with food and music way beyond hunger
or pain.

It is no surprise that the blues followed a crazy path
from slave ships anchored in terrible southern harbors
all the way to bars in Mississippi, Chicago and New Orleans.

It was in how Gertrude "Ma" Rainey resurrected the image
of a woman losing her man, and Bessie Smith became
the undisputed Empress of all Delta Blues teaching us that
sorrow always holds hands with love.

The Reverend Gary Davis moved gods and goddesses
that slept inside the temple of our bones to shake loose
lashes of lightning in the form and shape of dance moves
that exhilarated the soul and set us free to traverse the sweet
corridors of flight over and over again.

Blind Lemon Jefferson strummed notes that rose and fell
on wings of desire until all of us came to believe
there was going to be light at the end of that blind man's
tunnel.

Robert Johnson stood at the crossroads and called
to all of us to shake free of whatever binds a soul
and move outside the confines of a life to touch
the splendid body of a morning that night had spent
hours undressing.

When I walk down to the blowhole that sits at the edge
of the ocean and listen to the rise and fall of waves
that signal a new day, I hear a background of blues

snaking its rhythms past slavery's chains and alcohol fueled
visions. I move into the realm of blood, sweat and tears
of future generations that gives birth to an elemental jive,

a smoky infusion beginning and ending in some feast of notes
where we all sit down together, loosen our clothes and feel
the ship dock in that lonesome harbor.

This must be how the blues resurrects the misbegotten, forgotten,
disappeared, and abandoned heartache that resides in our terrain
of ghosts. The place for marginalized voices to gather with their
sheet music for the newly risen so that choral reckoning
we have been waiting for all our lives can finally happen.

Mississippi 4 AM

It was 4 AM and you were staring out
the bedroom window. The water under
the Tallahatchie bridge was pulling you
up from sleep.

You woke hungry for crawfish you could suck
out of the shell with your tongue and teeth.
Trucks were forming a line at that yellow and red
Crawdad Hole sign just this side of Water Valley.

Everything was triggering something else
causing a rising tornado inside the bones of you
creating a flood water of lost souls pulling you out
to whole hog barbecue pits

where you found your Granddaddy sleeping off
an all-nighter by his fire-filled hand-dug hole
with the best meat-smoking coals this side of
Hattiesburg, Tupelo, or Memphis, Tennessee

creating a hunger road that began in your knees
and caused you to beg forgiveness for every
broken promise you ever made, caused you to
throw back the hand sewn quilt that covered
the tops of pines and redbuds until the smell of trees

became the smell of sex, became the smell of fire,
became the smell of tar-laid roads and fresh cut
switch sticks left in a pile on top of a refrigerator
just waiting for the hand of your mother to grab one up

and chase you through the field of yellow weeds
that inhabit your arms and legs, until you are slipping
and sliding down the sides of some velvet ditch

a fortune teller warned you to watch out for.
You are in Mississippi now she laughed. *You are
conjuring the dead. You are playing poker with a Voo-Doo Queen.*

You are dreaming about tar paper shacks and
bedspring blues, match box blues, rain-smeared blues.
Baby ghosts are threading their way
through bayous and swamps you are running through,

filled with pain and the soul-searching face of some
old woman you swear belongs to your grandmother,
your sister, or to you.

But here you are, 4 AM, searching for redemption
on your hands and knees in the dust broken floor
of your *Sunday School Go-to-Meeting* mind

where every hand-clapping song has the
gap-toothed grin of someone you were dying
to love, but who was never able to find their way

out of heartache's bed, long enough
to love you back again.

The Swimmers

Sometimes for no reason I drive to the river
to sit at the edge watching morning unfold. Soon
the swimmers arrive and strip their clothes off
unashamed to be so exposed to the world.

They pull on slick wetsuits, so they resemble seals
and stand around laughing and talking with each other
as though they are a family of water creatures sharing this
language of the deep only they understand.

I imagine they are getting ready to resume their sojourns with water,
with the clear undulation that is river song, river wind,
river light, all of it together now becoming river mind.
They will pull handfuls of the river from in front of their bodies,
pressing it behind them, forming a wake, while they swim
the long green body of this snake.

Soon they disappear, taking the soft round curve
that stretches like endless hope at the edge of water
and leaves foam pearling her necklaces against the shore.
I can imagine swimming the rich wetness with them,
pulling the minerals of water against my face, tasting
the salt of her body with my tongue, laying my ear down
again and again just to listen to the heartbeat of the land
as it surfaces from so deep a place, as it wraps their bodies
in this perfect sound of water moving her great currents
across the land.

Mapping

When I drive the long road from my country life headed
to the nearest hip adrenaline bursting city, I pass through
small towns and the long-whispered stretches defined by
forgotten lives that once inhabited and thrived there.

I think of mapping it all, this land filled with her quotient of
imbedded trauma, tattooed with her own haphazard markers;
abandoned farms, broken down gas stations, *falling back to earth* barns.
I think of them all as small buoys of light floating in what otherwise
is the darkness that swells and dips and creates an ocean we all share.

Lately I want to map everything. How I left home. Why I turned left
there and didn't go right. Why I chose a freeway instead of the scenic
route. Who was I back then? Where were you? Did we know
on some cellular *trapped in space* level we were headed

like two planets inexplicably drawn toward one another's
gravitational pull? Behind me my mother is still standing in the back
of her kitchen canning tomatoes, parceling out simple phrases
that stick like wildfire in my throat. *Know who you are. First and
foremost. Everything else will fall into place.* Words I packed in my suitcase
and set on the shelf of every house I ever lived in, mapping my
course, trying to make sense of it all.

Inviting Death In

I ran into a neighbor this morning
in line in the coffee shop taking a break
from tending a dying loved one.

It made me think how easily death slips in
when we least expect. No matter the
time or year, death is such a patient player,

always conscious of how he is dressed for the occasion
so that when he finally arrives, we are always surprised
by his attire; a three-piece suit, cowboy chaps,
or a sequined dress if he decides to come in drag.

Sometimes he sits and cries with us, sometimes he has
that macho swagger, wearing too tight jeans, signaling
that although he may once have been insecure

now he is ready to grab hold of whatever he can
lay his hands on. Evenings I sit in front of the fire
and try to imagine welcoming him in, even though

he is not really expected to arrive for years. I imagine him
at the foot of our bed when you are tracing the slick wet reaches
of my body, tracing the curve of bones rising out of their
sleep-filled dark, asking where am I?

I smell the scent of his hair, wild rose or orchid.
I imagine standing naked before him, in this body
made of earth and sorrow, made of dreams and ancient
ancestor vowels, filled with all the fine dark tributaries of the soul.

I imagine standing like that, stripped bare, unashamed
of anything I have ever done, while he just sits, speechless,
and stares.

Mendocino Shuffle

Because I live in a small town I sometimes try to pass
as a tourist, which means wearing a hat and dark glasses
to the bakery, post office, gas station and grocery store.

I don't fool anyone. I am still the *slow on the tongue* story
of one more local woman trying to make loose ends meet,
carrying one more whiff of sea wind in her hair,
and the words *shoulda   coulda   woulda* trapped
mid-way in her throat.

Our children grew into adults thinking this small slice of life
was the entire world and jumped trains, hitched rides or
boarded planes to far reaches in their hurry to over-compensate
for being raised in the *we know everything about who you are world*
of small-town manifestos.

It sometimes feels like we are all the same congregation
of the earth, of the rural speak, brigade of the firefly wish-makers,
praying for rain to start or stop, raising money by racing each other
on the beach in "years old, too tight shorts" or gathering to pick up
bright plastic traces of left behind parties from sand dunes
we refer to as home.

Perhaps it all comes down to that Mendocino Shuffle,
the angle of our small-town sex; slow to come, hard to disengage
from or remain engaged to, yet always sweetly addictive
on the tongue.

Ides of March

May is sitting in the back corner of the garden
patient beyond reason for the cold dip of January
to move on. A fox sits on top of the compost bin,
lean, hopeful for a coming spring. I can see the outline
of her ribs on the side of her chest. She has been running
each morning from her new den to check the compost
for food once again.

I keep thinking we are stuck in the Ides of March,
the fox along with us, unable to move past the tragedy
of an unexpected attack, we are crouched in defensive mode
hunkered down with only the icy cold of winter's fingerprint
for sex.

It is hard to let myself be loved, hard to love back.
I carry the taste of aluminum against my tongue,
carry the unwanted hunger for something I cannot have.
But what that is, I don't know. I carry some bulbs
I am too angry to plant with enough compassion
to insure they will grow. If spring would just
move out of her protective stance against the half-broken fence,
I might feel able to work in the garden, prune back the wild roses,
make another stab at going on a dump run.

Freedom

Richie Havens is belting out the song
Freedom as though the song is all I've got left
to hang onto. He keeps repeating it
like a punch in the mouth, like a jab
on the arm, like a slap on the back,
reminding me not to fall into that
I'm too tired to keep on trying place I love
to sink into. I'm too sad, I'm too overwhelmed
I'm too lonely, I'm too caught up in my heart-sick blues
to even think about anyone else. But Richie
is belting it out, growly and scratchy and
pounding and relentless like a real force
of nature. He's conjuring something
strong enough for me to hang onto,
conjuring past abuse into present injustice
and throwing the whole mess into the future.
Like a sucker punch, like a wake-up call
to reach out, step out, grab hold because, after all,
freedom is all we've got left
to help us get through.

Heart Failure

When the long curving silence of Highway 128
When the day slowed into something unfathomable
When the wind kept blowing pale yellow leaves
When we were the only ones left in the world
When you pulled the car over to the edge
When you would not let me drive
When you said you only wanted to stop for a moment
When the day slowed into something unfathomable
When I felt the world descend in huge silence
creating her bell shape around us
When I asked if you were going to be alright, *is everything ok?*
When you answered look how beautiful the yellow leaves
like small birds drifting in air
When you would not let me drive
When the world descended around the two of us
in her bell shape
When your heart slowed to one beat
When you finally asked for help
When we were the only ones left in the world

The Morning We First Met

You like to tell the story how you won me over.
Not with flowers, although you are good at flowers,
not with those tiny foil stars you filled an envelope with
and left in the front seat of my car so when I got off work,
hot and tired, exhausted from teaching all day, I could open
an unmarked envelope and spill hundreds of shiny red
or gold stars across my lap.

No, you like to say it was because
you offered me a place to take a shower.
It was the storm season, and I had been without power
for two weeks washing my privates as my mother
and her sisters would say, in a bowl of water
I heated on the stove and keeping a basketful
of dirty laundry in the backseat of my car
whenever I went to town in hopes soon the
power at the laundromat would also be
restored.

We said hello standing in line at the local grocery
and when I told you I was one of the ones
whose power was still not on
you invited me to do my laundry at your place
and said I could also take a shower since
I was already going to be there.

I remember following your car up the long hill
that led to a single dad's house, bikes in the yard,
basketball hoop in the driveway, wondering
what I was doing going to your house for a shower,
but two weeks without power and you find yourself
gladly accepting someone's offer of hot water.

You gave me a clean towel, had coffee ready
when I finished. We sat in your living room,
a little breathless, afternoon sun was letting me know
it was soon going to be time to go.

The part of the story I like to tell is the part
where I knew this was going to be the beginning
of something extraordinary. I remember feeling
a small twirling somewhere inside my chest,

the feel of that movement inside my body
like a crazy dancer was the damndest thing,
something jumping around inside me like that,
while I sat, trying not to look too long into your eyes,
concentrating as best I could on sipping your coffee
in a dark blue mug.

Queen Bitch

Taking the dog for an evening walk I follow him
off-road into the woods. I bend low to squeeze my body
through this network of branches but keep going.
The dog running ahead disappears up a small hill
heavy with thorny vines.

I am going deeper now, reminding myself to notice signs
when I need to find my way back out. Just when I pause
to untangle blackberry thorns, there she is; amazing Queen-

of-my-compost-bin fox, and she is standing at the small bend
just ahead measuring her lead time if she must run, but
why isn't she running, why did she want to be seen?

Her fur is matted and wet near her stomach. Was she just nursing
her kits? She is totally the Queen Bitch of all foxes I have ever seen.
A neighbor used to leave open cans of dog food in her backyard
every evening, so in the falling twilight she could watch them,

a male and female jumping and playing through the field
headed straight to that dog food. My bitch doesn't need
canned anything, you can see it in her eyes, she is a survivor,
way-wise beyond her foxy years.

Garden Elegy

Last night an unexpected burst of cold
arrived from Alaska's deranged mind
and swept through the garden leaving behind
a trail of tears.

Petals were stripped from every petal bearing
thing which had assumed it was safe to bloom
and preen and dazzle the world with
random color.

Branches filled with fat apple blossoms
were broken and hanging like bedraggled corpses
from the mother tree.

I walked to the far edge of the property
where everything is wild and found a sunny spot
to sit and grieve.

But then I realized the wildness
all around me was untouched,
seemed stronger with its sprint of frigid air,
as if it was saying
is that all you've got? Bring it on, I'm ready.

The ruins of the garden I created lay in their scattered
shapes surrounded by this wilderness at all the edges,
this clue to survival, this ancient untranslatable
in the here and now world, but roughly meaning
everything was working out as planned.

Archeology of Us

Some mornings when I roll over in bed
and find your head tucked mid-way
between my chest and pelvis to feel
the soft brush of your hair against
the borders of my body, and your voice
rising in morning air like a wingless ghost
created from the simple firmament
of our bodies, whispering indecipherable
untranslatable words, it is as though
we are meeting for the first time
tangled up in night's long boat
of storms and drownings
of surviving months lost at sea
and I am surprised by the fathomless
depths of this love, growing silver at
all the edges, growing deeper into
the mines of my body, this
archeological dig we began
a lifetime or more ago.

Soul of the Thing

The afternoon I finally invite you in
my daughter asks if you know how
to play chess. Accustomed to our
single mother daughter *it's us
against the world* stance, she decided to see
if you could match her twelve-year-old strategies
for determining if my new boyfriend would last.

At the end of that game, she understood
that unlike the previous boyfriend she referred to
as a woodchuck, you did have chess playing capabilities.
That was the mouth of our rivers joining, your two boys
and my girl forming tributaries of some elemental thing.
Beneath the surface of our waters, an algorithm was forming,
that seemed to explain the warp and weft of those mingled lives.

Indescribable with words it was "our pod" the way
we all came to depend on one another, the way
we created our currents of connectedness.
Our map of survival was there, as we remained
steadfastly separate, yet connected, as remarkable
in our losses as our gains, touched by something incandescent,
on the horizon creating something light bearing in our
tough as nails yet tender to the touch
soul of the thing.

Runaway Horses

Sometimes you want to ride the runaway horses.
They come at odd hours. Sometimes wake you from sleep
kick-starting your day with hoofbeats inside your head.

The moon has risen above the earth's veiled outline
and you are waiting for the herd of wild mustangs
to come thunder-clapping across the plains of your mind.

You smell them first. Wild horse scent that invades your body
and causes you to remember one night in Texas in the dead
of summer after a day so hot the grass still carried the spell

of heat in all her blades and every time your bare feet moved
through them there was that green heat smell rising like
a southern ghost trailing after you. There was a party
your family was famous for, sad cousins and frightening uncles
moving through all the rooms of your house.

There were knots of people dancing on the breezeway
sliding their feet through salt your father sprinkled there
since it reminded him of his years in the nightclub business.
You were drinking gin and tonics one of your brothers
kept sneaking to you and someone said let's get the guns
out of the closet and shoot them in the backyard.

I watched my brothers take the hinges off the door, lay it gently
against the wall and hand out the rifles our father kept locked away
from all of us. We slipped out the back door and someone shouted
they bet they could hit a car and someone else said we could all
have a turn shooting into the trees and the grass felt scratchy
against my bare legs when I stood leaning against one of my brothers

and pressed the rifle against my shoulder
like it belonged there, thinking how it felt good
to be doing something at night outside that house,
like shooting those rifles into the dark woods
and never knowing if you hit something or not.

Big River Adagio

Twilight at Big River beach and pelicans are circling tidal pools
searching for a safe place to drift and dream in the coming dark.
Anxious to empty the day's thoughts and leave them as footprints
to be washed out to sea, I walk barefoot on the sand.

The light is filled with that soft familiar voice that acts as
intermediary between night and day, but I feel the old
sorrow for no reason that rises and falls in sea wind
and seems to permeate the air and belong to this rocky shore
and in belonging to the shore also belongs to me.

I think of the family of all of us walking together
like this through twilight, opening some long-lost
book of the dead, trying to make sense of the
senseless puzzle that is the violent history
that permeates our lives

until all the diverse pieces of that puzzle are drawn
to fit themselves back together and abide with this other
uncanny feeling of something forever lost
or disappearing all around us.

It is the lay of the storm-washed rocks at the edge
of the cliffs that offer solace in their abiding grace
on the margins of water and land that can suddenly
bring me to my knees and remind me there is

still time to be a part of the cartography
of surprising possibilities in this lowering dark.
I can sit awhile and allow the voices from the past and present
to create a tapestry of lives that offer comfort in this
cold Pacific air and perhaps like the pelicans,

seek a haven, quiet my questions of why or what for,
by drifting into the space that nature offers,
in the folds of her dark blue tent.

Bodhisattva Blues

Thank you for letting me stay at your house,
for using the last of your eggs. It felt sacrilegious
making coffee in mugs that could have come from
great distances I would never know, placing my lips
on rims that might have travelled from the Azores
or perhaps just the Walmart at the other end
of town. It didn't matter. It still felt as though
I was getting ready to drink sacred water. Thanks too
for the sheer inexplicable crazed beauty of your cat
curled in an apostrophe of prideful awareness of her
own strange behavior throughout the night, bouncing
up and down on the yoga mat on the floor at the foot
of your bed, where I imagined you standing, early morning light
streaming across your face and arms, hovering inside
the palms of your hands pressed against your heart
before you bend down to begin the ancient wise poses.
Thank you for allowing me to share your space and for
your neighbor who sits like a talisman of some dark
unknowable past on his *falling down too late to ever be fixed*
front porch, behind a long row of ten or more
shiny motorcycles lined up just in front of his house
forming a prayer to dead engines, creating an ecstatic psalm
for the wild portion of life he once straddled
but now has put the kickstand down on forever.
At dusk I walked outside beneath trees still humming with heat
and there he sat, perfect bodhisattva as though he had died
a million times already, as though the groove of his life
of failed intentions was imbedded so deeply in the warp
and weft of the world, he was bound to repeat the same old
mistakes again. This is just to say, please God of Engines and Guns,
God of Knives and Hard Knocks, after he passes over, please
don't send him back for one more go around.

Pardon his mistakes, pardon his losses
and hallucinatory schemes,
pardon him of every broken wing he carries
in his world-weary lap, because sitting like that
on the crumbling *memory of a porch*, with his long
flowing beard, and his hand raised to wave at me
when I smiled and walked past, was enough to answer
all my earthly questions of why or what for, it was enough
to fill all my empty lakes and calm all my tiny blue rivers
of pain or bewilderment with a strange quiet bodhisattva blues
all its own.

This Time Around

These days lost things surface in my dreams
like solar flares illuminating answers to all my
whys or *what fors*. They sizzle in the night sky
of my mind, like text messages from a god
grown bored with the usual life and death matters.
They sizzle and flare for an instant, while I try
to hold on to their features, reconstruct the past
bring lost things in a dream suitcase into the everyday
routines of my life; mornings with green tea
or afternoons with bread and honey.
Sometimes I unpack my grandmother's voice
insisting "this isn't so bad" as she changes the dressings
on my burned nine-year-old legs, lifting the gauze strips
she says "This isn't so bad. My mother drowned
in a tidal wave, now that was bad."
At night I dreamed about her mother, treading water
forever, never able to reach shore. That was when
I began to sleepwalk, seeking my own safe harbor,
trailing bandages like a lonely mummy through
all the rooms of my parents' house.
Lately it is my friend, Yousef, who surfaces out of breath
as though he has spent a lifetime swimming to find me,
just to say he lives in Canada. I know he is dead,
killed in a riot in Boxberg, South Africa all those years ago.
"You're crazy," he shouts at me, "I live in Canada" and then
I wake up. Light splinters wings across our legs.
The smell of night is still trapped in your hair
and I know I have been weaving dream blankets for our bed.
But who knows? Maybe Yousef is alive, is living a new life
in Canada. If I believed in reincarnation as he did,
I could believe he is there, living a new life, this time around
in the body of a girl and she is selling peaches

from her family farm, standing on some street corner
holding bright globes of color, lighting up the dark
that surrounds her features and covers
this world.

Ghosts Everywhere

The day before we leave Mississippi we drive
to Faulkner's anti-bellum mansion. He wrote
most of his work here saying there was plenty
enough for him to write about without ever having
to leave, so he was going to stay put.
Within sight in the backyard sits the slave quarters.
My daughter says look how small,
where are the windows? We walk around it
reading the plaque on the door that
states the last family of slaves to live there
numbered ten. That night at another fancy mansion
we eat shrimp and oysters and drink champagne.
A young woman next to me says it is very challenging
living here. There are ghosts, she says, there are ghosts
everywhere.

Holding On and Letting Go

Some mornings I tell myself
I am done with holding onto fear,
done with holding onto tears,
done with anger and grief,
silhouettes that have haunted me
for a lifetime
or more.

The truth is I just cannot hold anymore
inside my body. I am leaking at all my seams
and leaving a trail wherever I go.
How much are we supposed
to be able to hold anyway?

I can drive along the coast highway
and roll down all the windows and try
to let all those packed-to-the-gills things go,
send them off on their own journey
like kidnapped sailors finally set loose at sea.

They will have to find their own way, navigate by stars,
make up myths about the size and shape of the world,
dream about monsters in the deep. I don't care anymore.
I am going to become as empty as winter and dream
about the coming spring.

Visible Horizon

I repeat the names of birds on the endangered list.
Grebes, Snowy Plovers, Marbled Murrelets.
Bay area birds all close to saying goodbye forever.
Our environmentalist guide says repeating words for loss
is helpful as a reminder to ground ourselves in. She says
it is good practice to imagine ways you would call for help
in times of great crisis. I try making a list of ways to call
for help.
1. Try making smoke, use whatever materials are at hand
2. Hang shiny objects where they can swing and flash in the sun
3. Drape a big white sheet from a high vantage point
4. At night make fire not smoke
5. If you are in a boat hold a handmade torch as far away
   from the boat for as long as you can.
The environmentalist tells our little group it is not too late.
That it helps her to imagine looking for a visible horizon,
imagining one she has not yet seen, filled with
hopeful outcomes for the planet, for our
children's children. Sleeping in Sausalito that night
I dream about a distress call rising from the
sleeping ocean, arriving from as far away as Japan,
desperately seeking solid ground. Finally, a series
of flashing lights on the horizon
short short short long long long,
clearly signaling their repeated
SOS flashing light into my eyes
just before I wake up.

Groundswell   (for M.K.)

After the fire, the house was gone
but remained room after room in the ashes
we cupped inside our hands.

We lifted bits and pieces up to one another.
A melted toy took on great dimension.
A small green plant became miraculous
poking one leaf through a mound of ash.

Once this ground held our bedroom
where we met under cover of night,
tending small wounds left over
from day.

Here was the kitchen marked by
the shape of a melted spoon
curved into a perfect half-moon.

Suddenly, from the hillside above,
as though it has miraculously risen
resurrected from the burned ground

rising, music from one bird
sitting like a lone survivor
filling empty branches
with song.

Incantation for a Healing

I try on the leopard print strapless
bathing suit. I open the top part
and step down inside. I am sinking
into my mother's body
her wide pelvis, her strong hips
giving birth to eight children.
One by one they slip through
her body that is my body.
This is a healing, this is a sharing
this is her life I am swallowing the bones of.
I am pulling a leopard print bathing suit
up the tops of my legs past my grandmother's
dreams, blue stones in a windowsill
catching the sun, reflecting her eyes,
her house, her fields, her sorrows
her loves. We are together now as one.
She is slipping her body inside mine.
We are bending low to step into
a great grandmother's house
to build a fire to cook food. We are
drinking water from an ancestor's well,
this is a healing, this is a sharing.
I am pulling the suit up past my waist,
my waist is a curving bowl, a widening river
tributaries of my women, I am diving into.
Together we are swimming from death
into life, scattering molecules of breath like rain.
I am learning the spells, I am dreaming
I am receiving
I am gathering the voices
hiding in the forest of my body.
I am pulling a leopard print strapless

bathing suit up past my ribs, past fear,
past heart ache, threading the needle
with our lives, slipping out the portal,
this is desire, this is rage,
this is hopeless, this is hopeful.
This is the gift I am pulling up,
covering my breasts, opening my heart,
incensing their lives and mine.
I am carrying them all with me.
We are walking through the rooms
of my house. We are dancing.
We are wearing a leopard print
strapless bathing suit into
this day that together
we are all jumping into.

The Woman Remembers She is a River

> *How I miss the animals of the ocean,*
> *in the depths that can't be measured*
> *of my heart,*
> *deeper than water, or a universe of dark matter.*
> *I want mercy in this world....*
> 　　　　　Linda Hogan, *Mercy, The Word*

Dream Journal

There was a blue wooden dinghy. We left at dawn.
We wondered if our lives together would be enough.
We were searching for something larger than ourselves.
We were alone in that moment.
This is not my life you understand.
This searching, this boat, this dream of us
and them. There was a storm, children gathered
in tight knots in their mother's arms.
Many languages surfaced for the word help.
There was an understanding that rose
from outside the boat, *that we were alone,*
that defined with perfect clarity
this scene. This moment was all we had.
Time was precious, was parceled out in cups.
On the horizon, a rocky shore, the infinite possibility of
begin again with empty hands waited just ahead.

Suminagashi. *(for S.R.)*

My daughter is teaching
                         suminagashi. That ancient art
             of Japanese marbling of ink from water onto paper
                       "floating ink."
This is a dance.
               I hold my breath
above my tray of water.
                     I lift my eyes to
the woman who sits across from me.
                         She is whispering something
to her brush, a prayer, I think.
            She is slowly swirling her brush
into her water.
            There are six of us
                    around a table.
My daughter directs
               the calm flow
that envelops the room.
                Just outside a sandwich truck
      is waiting.
Soon we will all
            lay our brushes down
walk outside.
                    There are dark pink blossoms
waiting for us.
There are blossoms
           everywhere
in this part of Berkeley.
                   We carry suminagashi
in our minds with us across the street.
             We all move like our brushes
hovering above the water
          delicately allowing the wind

      to float against our bodies.

Greece

I was alone in a country I did not speak the language of.
Language floated by me in the street.
Beautiful figures of words in transparent coats glided by.
They whispered to me as they passed
and I smiled at the sound their tongues made
against their teeth, because I was lonely
but I was not sad. I walked at dawn into the hills
above the town and the wind tried to trap me
in the sound of the sea and birds flew up
in sudden excited explosions and everything felt
untouchable.
Once a woman came towards me on the trail
riding a donkey with bells tied around its neck.
She stopped and motioned for me to climb up
behind her. She offered me her hand and pulled me up.
We did not need to speak. I rode behind
her all the way down to where the ocean
tried to climb the side of the island where someone
once told me Odysseus had lost his way listening
to the songs of sirens. I rode on the back of a donkey
wearing a necklace of bells and was filled
with the language of that land.

Moonglow Over the Rio Hondo

I did not know moonlight could lift a snowy field
into the hand of God. If the hand of God is Nature,
then it abides in the form and shape of the every day.

It becomes a broken branch drifting downstream,
awash with sunlight, slips into the smell of rain,
transforms into an echo of thunder
gathering her dark gray skirts
at the edges of sight or lays her body down into
the form and shape of a burned shoulder of hill
with one patch of green left behind as a testament to life.

Perhaps this is the juncture where an ancestor
whispering our secret names steps forth with a voice
stretching across time and space, to calm our litany
of questions with a murmuration of answers
in the rising songs of starlings
or the settled moments of doves.

If moonglow over the Rio Hondo can rise
to spread across the cheekbones of this land,
signaling hope or despair or welcoming
a single note of bird song, then our lives
can be filled with the endless possibilities
that nature offers in wood, water, air or fire.

Because our lives are painted
into mysterious circles of completion,
spinning us into mandalas of stars,
we can return again and again
to an archeology of hope

and sit as still as an estuary
filled with the quiet reckoning
that water and moonlight
offer to the soul of a thing.

We can stare across sleeping fields
and watch the everyday transform
into the miraculous. In the distance
one egret rises into the air, impermanent

as an after-thought of day, signaling
a sharp intake of breath coming to rest
in our lungs as life-force that fills
our bodies with wonder
and joins us all as one.

Welcoming The New Year

Winter arrived two nights ago
staggering up the coast road
as though she had never come
this far West and was unsure
how to go.

But she is here now,
triangulating sadness and joy
into a language filled with absence.

The old year is going to bed
and from my porch
I can hear the surf
swallowing the beach,

can smell the jasmine
that still blooms unaware
that tomorrow her white petals
will have frozen into an unbearable shape

of beauty, so fragile it will last
for only one day
of our lives.

The world is still dancing
her own tango of give and take.
We go to bed with nightmares
of war, the new list of extinct birds
has been released, and social media
keeps telling us guns are a necessity for life.

But we are still able to sit
in the rising light of the world
and know the true nature
of a place we call home.

This year I want to plant a garden
of every mistake, every sorrow
I cannot let go, every piece of anger and hurt
carried over from the past

so I can nurture some new growth,
watch flowering unfold as part
of the coming year.

If I must name it, I call it
everything that has happened
for an unknown reason,
that is misunderstood,
that cradles some undefined tragedy,

will be put to rest in this garden
to grow into something green,
and if I am lucky, will give shade
in the heat of summer
where I can lay down in the grass
and listen to the heartbeat of the world.

Twenty-Two States on the Other Side of Life

You must be twenty-two states
on the other side of life by now.
Must be the echo of home
in the minds of sailors lost at sea.
You must be cracking jokes
at the bar in the other world
falling drunk in the land
of the disappeared
trying to become a by-gone
in the here and now minds
of the rest of us you left behind.
You must be an uncontrollable ghost
in all the elbows of air
that like to settle their arms
around my shoulders
first thing in the morning
and last thing at night.
This is to say I am missing you
but learning to cope.
I am wanting more and settling for less.
I am catching handfuls of you
in rainstorms, wringing fistfuls of you
out of my hair.
I am rocking on your porch
in the mountains outside Taos,
seventy-two hours straight,
counting the range of ghost trails
your solar shape flares
on summer nights
just overhead.

Disappearing

It begins in the need to fall into silence.
Our guide says go slow, allow your body to open
step away from everything you brought with you
that you have learned to define yourself by.

I imagine letting go of the house, notice
the mortgage payment slipping away into blue air.
Concentrate on placing your feet on the path
in front of you, her voice becoming a beacon of light.

She is disappearing into trees just ahead. Imagine
you are having a conversation with these trees,
her voice floats out of leaves.

I am still imagining letting go, the dog, the cat,
all the physical things that bind me to a time and place
are floating now in air.
I imagine holding my husband's face in my hands
then his hand reaching for mine
before he disappears.

I am alone. Let your body go, I hear
the guide's voice from somewhere green
still out of sight. There is the sound of a heartbeat
that appears to come from the trees.

There is the sound of slow breathing that appears
to belong to me. The guide's voice drifts from out of
one hundred shades of green. "Trust the ground
beneath your feet," she says.

Trust this silence, trust this heartbeat
just trust.

Pleiades

I don't know why they are the ones I always search for,
those seven sisters. Lakota say they went out to play
and were spotted by giant bears who chased them.
Those sisters were smart, they climbed on top
of a large rock, Devil's Tower, in Wyoming and prayed
to the Great Spirit to save them.
Their prayers were powerful and that rock grew too steep
for those bears. The rock kept going until it touched the
sky and the sisters all became stars.
I like the part about all the sisters staying together,
living like that untouchable in the sky.
I like the part about being chased by bears,
about the rock growing into the sky.

Note: The Seris from Northwest Mexico saw the Pleiades as seven women about to give birth. (Source: *Comcáac quih yaza quih hant ihíip hac: Diccionario seri-español-inglés* by Mary B. Moser and Stephen A. Marlett.) The Monache people from the Sierra Nevada region, tell the constellation as six wives who loved onions more than they loved their husbands. The Nez Perce, from the Pacific Northwest area, also tells a tale of the constellation as seven sisters, one of which fell in love with a mortal and was so aggrieved by his death that she pulled the sky over her face, which is why she is so hard to see while her sisters burn bright. (Source: *Indian Legends of the Pacific Northwest* by Ella Clark.)

We Heard Water

We heard water calling our names,
heard her throat open wider than
fifty states strung out together
and she woke us at 3 a.m. calling our names.

She was so old she lost the thread
in those conversations, half-finished sentences
floated on her waves and currents.
Phrases came through like, *trees are wandering lost on the horizons*
toxins are eating up all the blue.

Stars are so sad they have forgotten
how to live in night's soft dark.
Birds are dropping out of the sky,
dead are piling up at the gates of dreams

and we ask what are we supposed to do?
Water answers with her great rushing sigh,
that sound that means she is done with us.
Maybe she had just been calling our names
to wake us up out of our lives. She wanted to shake
sleepwalking out of us. Maybe she really had
the thread all along in those midnight conversations.

Maybe she was telling us we were the answer
and all we had to do was go deeper, go slower,
learn to flow, crawl on our bellies
for miles if we have to.

The Angel of Life

There were water birds at the edges of sight.
There was a cold fist of winter air.
There was the smell of smoke, the taste of ashes
in the back of her throat.
In the back of her throat there was
a great sadness, sitting by a fire she built
in a forest clearing.

The angel of life was standing at the water's edge.
The angel of life had one broken wing and was fishing
for sunlight on stones, trying to decipher
the meaning of everything that was lost.

The angel liked the smell of smoke
inside the woman's throat, liked sitting
in the Yolla Bolly wilderness,
liked swimming in the Eel River.

The woman held the smell of green.
She imagined running away with the angel of life.
They would sleep in boxcars, and huddle under bridges.
They would drink rain.
She imagined archipelagos inside all her waterways.
She wanted to be the shoreline and carry the language of waves.
The slight noise of water birds and the soft scratch of shells
on the bottoms of her feet reminded her there was something
waiting beyond the horizon if only she would begin
walking towards it.

Water Binds Me to You

Rivers bind me to you with their names
        Yampa Tigris Euphrates White Red Colorado Snake
              Oceans bind me to the blind speech of your past
    the weight of that grief
              manifested in the violent history of this land
  To listen to water, I lay my ear next to sand
        secrets flood my body with their ebb and flow
    Water binds me to you
           How many rivers have carried the bodies of the
massacred
    rocked souls to sleep or set dreamers free
      past the color of their skin or sexual longing
        all the way to the ending place where spirits
scatter
          like seeds in wind and water traces her lifeline in rings
              that turn a planet blue
       I stand at the edge of the Pacific and repeat the words
    as though there is no distinction between dream
and instinct
        as though I can contain all this wild blue longing
          by saying the names
    Yampa Tigris Nile Euphrates White Red Colorado
  Snake
     Russian Eel Little River Big River
Navarro   Albion

What Abides

I did not know I still carried the Southwest inside me,
the architect of people's faces carved by wind
etched in despair, tangled up in love, hollowed by loss.

I could not know I carried the figure of a boy
hanging from the top rung of the water tank
in O'Neal's field, wearing his sister's dress.

How his longing to be a girl lives inside me.
How he was never accepted by his family, his friends, his world.
How he pulled his sister's dress on before he climbed the rungs
of that water tank to end his life.

But there he is. I lay him to rest now, I bless his body
and cut him free of the rope where he swings
inside the landscape I carry.

I did not know this was the ecology of loneliness.
Sitting at dinner last night a US Marshall talked
about chasing someone.

*"I tell you what…I put a gun to his ear and he
came with me no questions asked"*
I did not know the structure of lives is always
so close to the edge of things that any moment
we may topple over.

That sometimes there is no place to land.
That sometimes what abides is all
we have been given.

Return To Taos

Something about this landscape
brings out the untamed part
that lives inside you
brings out the wide-open mouth of sex
by the side of a hidden hot springs
at the base of a cliff
you had to hike down to.
Brings out a snowfall
with flakes too beautiful to be real
soft and brave at the same time.
Something in the air is so unafraid
that you are pulled out of yourself
to stand in the blue twilight
of a mesa at peace with black rocks
and red dirt.
The wind speaks to you about place,
time, people, and creates a connection
that inhabits the bones of your mouth,
the bones of your feet and hands
the difficult bones of your heart.
That sings a song only you understand
where the afternoon makes love with
you, and you belong to the eyes and hands
of every man, woman, and child
you pass in the street.
This is not a dream, this is the smell
of returning home, this is the wisdom,
the wanting, the waiting,
this is the wilderness of yourself.
This is your wounded body
being healed, with the antidote
that has always lived inside you
rising in a rush

through all the dark veins
of life, so you feel the doorways
in the deepest part of you opening
and finally understand
who you really are.

Becoming The Street

I wanted to become the street at night.
It was a strange craving, no reason
no plan behind the thought, just suddenly
I wanted all the passing shapes to fill me up.
Wanted that girl with twenty-two braids
her sister worked all morning on,
wanted that boy with the ripped
t-shirt zooming past on his clackety skateboard
wanted the cracks in the sidewalk
with their broken teeth smiles
wanted the old man tossing down a cigarette butt
wanted the woman who came along just then
and picked it up and still got her puffs.
I was ravenous for the street with her
smoke-streaked eyes and her torn neon dress,
her heels or bare feet.
I wanted the tents filled with people whose names
I didn't know but who called me sister anyway like
I was family every time I passed.
I wanted the hallways of the universe
to spill out her secrets in migrant tongues
so my pockets were filled
with so many languages my coat was
dragging on the ground and consonants and vowels
from the dispossessed and the possessed
were lingering in the corners
of all my joints. I wanted to lay down
in the music of *Round Midnight*
and listen to the pure song of the dark
hitching up her skirts, tightening
her belt, whistling some long-lost tune
that defined the simple shape of who we all are
and how becoming a street

can sometimes open
all the windows you thought
you nailed shut.

Finding a Cure for Cancer

That was the year everyone was driving to Mexico
to drink blue liquid or sometimes clear with
a snake's body curled in the fat part of the bottle.
We all appeared to have cancer and everyone
was asking everyone else if they had driven to
Mexico and seen the man in the white robe who
just sat all day in the shade under a little umbrella
and welcomed all the people lining up who had come
from all over the world for his cancer cure. There was an
old woman some of my friends went to who held their
heads in both of her hands while they cried. One by one
they came back and mostly didn't talk too much about
how the cure had worked for them or what it felt like
when the woman cradled their face in her hands.
I think her hands smelled like dirt or earth
after rain falls on it, or maybe they smelled
clean and ripe like persimmons and made you want to
lean back as far as your body could go, I mean really
lean back into the whole landscape of that part of the world
and plant yourself like a seed in the mind of those tough
southern hemisphere roots. I used to imagine
getting in my car and packing food in a cooler and
with the sound of bottles of water rolling around
on the floorboard just driving to one of those cancer curing
places. I used to imagine meeting the woman
with hands that smelled like rain in dirt
and how I would lean back, how I would fall
into some other world where the trees were filled
with birds singing songs in Spanish, where
I might even run into one of my friends
and we would both be wearing long robes
and we would not have to say anything to each other
but would be able to hold each other with our eyes

and when we smiled our teeth would be stained
through and through with the beautiful blue
dye in that cancer cure treatment.

Heartmoor

My friend says I am suffering from heartmoor.
*The primal longing for a home village to return to,
a place that no longer exists, if it ever did;
the fantasy of finding your way back home
before nightfall, a time when people
could still melt into a collective personality
and weren't just floating around
alone anymore.*
But this morning the smell of skunk
at the compost bin fills me with an unknown
nostalgia for something as primal
as a wild animal rooting through my
left over scraps of kale or tomatoes.
When my son describes
the unhoused person taking bites
from a whole cabbage at our local
grocery I am flooded by grief for
all of us, skunk rooting in thrown out
vegetable scraps, unhoused people searching
grocery aisles for anything edible,
ecstatic to find a cabbage.
Ditch-digger eating sandwich
by half-dug ditch, sunlight turning him
into a Van Gogh painting in his blue overalls
and sweat-stained bandana.
Wind at night waking the roof shingles.
Rain in her never satisfied *release and flow* refrain.
This must be me, filled with heartmoor
searching after nightfall, for my
path back home to a home that really
doesn't exist at all.

The Woman Remembers She is a River

The moment was swinging like a light in her arms
when she remembered she was a river.
The wind was creating havoc in the branches of her hair.
The tornado was dreaming spirals of cars and one or two
cows in her tunnel.

The rain was a hexagram of forgotten intentions.
The prayer was a small fist uncurling inside her mind,
her mind was awash with laundry to do and children
to care for when she remembered the tug and pull
of currents inside her womb,

when she remembered shore birds creating hieroglyphs
in her throat. The husband was calling her name,
the dog needed to go outside, the garden needed tending,
the goats needed milking when she remembered
the smell of salt in every wave and the bleak courage
of stones on her south facing riverbed.

The trapped moon inside her face sent fractured light
across her shore. The wood needed stacking,
the porch needed sweeping, the bills needed paying,
the cat needed stroking when she felt a generative wave
beginning in her toes,

when she remembered the beginning place
of seeking and finding
when she felt the lucky tide of infinite possibilities
crash through the doorway of her soul
and set loose the tsunami of herself and like a river
she was finally flowing into the sea.

ACKNOWLEDGEMENTS

Italicized lines in the first stanza of "Heartmoor" are quoted from the wonderful book, *The Dictionary of Obscure Sorrows* by John Koenig.

"Groundswell" is for Melania Kang.

"Suminagashi" is the ancient art of Japanese marbling and is for Solange Roberdeau.

"Moonglow over the Rio Hondo" was inspired by the original mixed media encaustic artwork, "Moonglow Over the Rio Hondo" by Taos artist, Nina Anthony.

Thanks to Wild Ocean Press for their dedication to poetry and to Robert Yoder, publisher and editor, who has worked with me on five books of poetry. Thanks also to Sharon Doubiago for her invaluable insight, suggestions and keen eye in editing. Gratitude to Fritz Horstman for use of his original art for the cover and many thanks to artist Solange Roberdeau for designing such beautiful book covers that always capture the essence of my poems. You are the best!

Special thanks to the Helene Wurlitzer Foundation for providing me such a beautiful space in which to create poetry. Thank you to Square Books in Oxford, Mississippi, and Gallery Books in Mendocino, California for hosting me as featured poet and for helping keep books alive. Thanks to Thacker Mountain Radio for featuring me in a live reading of "Blue Requiem" on your famous stage. And a shout-out to the Mendocino Community of Poets, and to the Fort Bragg, Ukiah, Point Arena, and Willits Poetry Series for their ongoing advocacy for poetry. Many thanks to Dan Roberts and the Rhythm Running River KZYX Poetry Program for continued support of my poetry on the air.

Thank you to my family for always having my back.

To Barry, as ever and always, soul-mate and best friend.

ABOUT THE AUTHOR

Devreaux Baker is the first Poet Laureate of Mendocino County and a recipient of the PEN/Oakland Josephine Miles Poetry Award for her book, *Red Willow People*. She has published six books of poetry and her poems have been widely published in many journals and anthologies including ZYZZYVA, Crab Orchard Review, A Paris Review, Feminist Studies in Religion, Poetry In Flight, Anthology in Celebration of El Tecolote, and the Canary Journal. She produced the Voyagers Radio Program of Original Student Writing for KZYX Public Radio and teaches poetry and creative writing in national and international workshops. Her Awards and Honors include the 2024 Willie Morris Award for Southern Writing in Poetry, the 2024, 2019 and 2014 Barbara Mandigo Kelly Peace Poetry Prize from the Nuclear Age Peace Foundation, the 2024 Steve Kowit Poetry Award, the 2022 Fischer International Prize for Poetry, the 2016 US Poets in Mexico Award, the 2012 Hawaii Council for Humanities International Poetry Prize, the 2010 Women's Global Leadership Poetry Prize, and a 1998 California Arts Council Award. She is a MacDowell Fellow, a Helene Wurlitzer Foundation Fellow, and a Hawthornden Castle Fellow. She currently produces the Mendocino Poets Reading Series at the Mendocino Art Center and is publisher of Wayfind Press.

Devreaux Baker lives in Northern California.

Website: www.devreauxbaker.org

www.ingramcontent.com/pod-product-compliance
Lightning Source LLC
Chambersburg PA
CBHW061804070526
44586CB00023B/2710